BOOK ANALYSIS

By William Norman

Cloud Atlas

by David Mitchell

DAVID MITCHELL

- **Born in Southport (England) in 1969.**
- **Notable works:**
  - *Ghostwritten* (1999), novel
  - *number9dream* (2001), novel
  - *The Thousand Autumns of Jacob de Zoet* (2010), novel

David Mitchell grew up in Worcestershire, England, and studied English and American literature at Kent University. He spent eight years teaching English in Japan before settling in Ireland with his wife and two children. Mitchell's writing might generally be categorised as 'contemporary fiction', but it often includes elements of the supernatural and fantastic, blending contemporary with science fiction and historical fiction. His debut novel, *Ghostwritten*, won the John Llewellyn Rhys Prize for the best work of British literature written by an author under 35, and *number9dream* and *Cloud Atlas* were both shortlisted for the Man Booker Prize.

As well as his seven novels, Mitchell has also written two opera libretti, contributed to the script of season two of the Netflix series *Sense8* (2015-2018) and translated *The Reason I Jump: One Boy's Voice from the Silence of Autism* (2007) by Naoki Higashida (Japanese writer, born in 1992) from Japanese into English (in collaboration with K. A. Yoshida).

CLOUD ATLAS

SIX OVERLAPPING STORIES IN ONE NOVEL

- **Genre:** novel
- **Reference edition:** Mitchell, D. (2014) *Cloud Atlas*. London: Sceptre.
- **1st edition:** 2004
- **Themes:** fate, the soul, connectivity, truth, oppression, predacity, apocalypse

Cloud Atlas is a novel which is made up of six separate but linked stories, five of them told in two parts, with the sixth, central story, in one piece. Each story begins but is interrupted by the next, during the course of which the new main character reads, watches or listens to sections of the previous story. After the sixth story, each of the others is revisited in reverse order, and each ends with the protagonist gaining access to the second half of the story that had been interrupted when their own began in the first place, so that the work ends with the same story it opened with. *Cloud Atlas* was well-received by critics and won several prizes, including the Richard and Judy Best Read of the Year, as well as being shortlisted for the Man Booker Prize, establishing Mitchell as one of the leading British authors of the early 21st century.

SUMMARY

THE PACIFIC JOURNAL OF ADAM EWING

Cloud Atlas begins with the 19th-century diary of a notary from San Francisco who finds himself stranded in the South Pacific following a storm. While awaiting repairs to the ship he is travelling on he meets an Englishman, Dr Goose, whose company he enjoys, and also witnesses the flogging of a slave, Autua, in a tribal village. When the ship sets sail, Autua reveals that he has stowed away on board and earns himself a place among the crew. Meanwhile, Ewing becomes increasingly ill, and is tended personally by Dr Goose.

LETTERS FROM ZEDELGHEM

In 1931, Robert Frobisher recounts, in the form of letters to his lover Rufus Sixsmith, his stay at the Belgian home of a reclusive and temperamental composer, Vyvyan Ayrs. Frobisher becomes Ayrs' amanuensis, writing his melodies into musical notation (as Ayrs' declining health has left him unable to do so himself), and their collaborations are successful. Frobisher finds a damaged copy of *The Pacific Journal of Adam Ewing* and deduces that Ewing is being slowly poisoned by the avaricious Dr Goose, but the second half of the book is missing. Meanwhile, Ayrs' wife, Jocasta, initiates an affair with Frobisher, although he soon seems to regret it and is anxious to hide it from the distrustful daughter of the house, Eva.

HALF-LIVES – THE FIRST LUISA REY MYSTERY

Set in 1975 and written in the style of a thriller, a would-be investigative journalist, Luisa Rey, stumbles across the scoop of a lifetime when she meets the elderly Rufus Sixsmith, an atomic physicist working at a nuclear power plant, Swannekke. He hints that there is a high risk of a deadly explosion occurring at the plant, but is murdered before they can meet again. Rey then finds an envelope of the letters Frobisher sent Sixsmith in his hotel room. She investigates Swannekke further and is taken into confidence by another scientist, Isaac Sachs, though she arouses the suspicions of two security men, elderly Joe Napier and ruthless Bill Smoke. She finds a copy of Sixsmith's report, hidden in her car by Sachs, but then has her car forced off a bridge by Smoke.

THE GHASTLY ORDEAL OF TIMOTHY CAVENDISH

In the present day, Timothy Cavendish has recently become the publisher of an unlikely bestseller, following the murder of a critic by the book's gangland author, Dermot Hoggins, which generated an unprecedented level of publicity for the book. Cavendish is also the recent recipient of half a manuscript for a thriller called *Half-Lives*. However, Hoggins' family seeks a share of the spoils, leaving Cavendish in debt and a great deal of trouble. He turns to his exasperated brother for help, who offers him a place to lay low: a hotel called Aurora House. Cavendish soon realises that all is not as it seems: Aurora House is actually a care home run by the sadistic Nurse Noakes and her henchman Withers, the groundsman, and he is little more than a prisoner there, his independence signed away. This realisation leads him to suffer a stroke.

AN ORISON OF SONMI~451

In a distant future, an 'orison' records Sonmi~451's face and words for posterity as she answers an archivist's questions. Sonmi~451 was one of 12 'fabricants', or clones, living and working as servers in an underground fast food chain called Papa Song's. Influenced by a fellow fabricant, Yoona~939, Sonmi~451 'ascended' to independent thought and was plucked from the restaurant and taken to a university for study. There she was able to develop her own mind freely under the protection of Professor Mephi and a postgrad student, Hae-Joo Im. In the middle of watching an ancient film, *The Ghastly Ordeal of Timothy Cavendish*, they are interrupted by enforcers storming the university.

SLOOSHA'S CROSSIN' AN' EV'RYTHIN' AFTER

In a post-apocalyptic world, hundreds of years after a cataclysmic event known as the Fall, Zachry tells his children about the annihilation of his childhood home and tribe on Hawaii by savage Kona warriors when he was a teenager. In the months before the Kona attack, Zachry's family host a researcher from a distant civilisation, Meronym. She tells Zachry that in the whole world, devastated as it is by nuclear and climatic destruction, only a few isolated and primitive societies have survived at all. Zachry's tribe worship a goddess called Sonmi, whom Zachry sees speaking from Meronym's orison; Meronym explains that Sonmi was actually a human being who lived many years ago and was 'judased', but that her words became influential after her death. When his home is destroyed, Zachry flees with Meronym to a neighbouring island where, even after his death, his children continue to activate the orison and watch Sonmi's recording.

AN ORISON OF SONMI~451

After escaping with Hae-Joo, Sonmi~451 is taken into hiding by the Union, an underground organisation opposing the Corpocracy. She visits a fabricant birthing facility, as well as a ship where older fabricants, believing they are about to be freed, are instead slaughtered to produce food for fabricants and consumers alike. Sonmi~451 records her *Declarations*, a declaration of rights for fabricants, before being captured by Corpocracy forces. She reveals that her entire 'ascension' and 'escape' was a fiction set up by the government to keep consumers afraid of fabricants but states that she believes in the long term her words will still lead to revolution. Before her execution, she asks to watch the rest of an old film...

THE GHASTLY ORDEAL OF TIMOTHY CAVENDISH

Awaking from his stroke, Cavendish sets about trying to escape from Aurora House. His initial attempts are foiled by Nurse Noakes, but with the help of three other inmates he finally comes up with a plan which does work, and in a dramatic jail-break they steal a car and drive to Scotland and freedom. Solvent again, Cavendish vows to write his own story into a bestseller and film; finally, the second half of the *Half-Lives* manuscript arrives for him to read and publish.

HALF-LIVES – THE FIRST LUISA REY MYSTERY

Rey survives the fall from the bridge and makes it to shore, but loses Sixsmith's report;

simultaneously, a jet with Sachs on board is destroyed by a bomb. When Rey returns home, she finds Napier there, but he persuades her that they are allies and that Smoke is the true danger. In a final showdown on Sixsmith's yacht, Smoke and Napier kill each other; Rey finds another copy of the report there and is finally able to get her scoop published. Sixsmith's niece sends Rey the rest of his letters from Zedelghem.

LETTERS FROM ZEDELGHEM

Ayrs begins to openly plagiarise Frobisher's work, and then reveals that he knows about Frobisher and Jocasta's affair and will ruin his career unless he cooperates. Frobisher runs away in the night, taking Ayrs' pistol from his room and the second half of *The Pacific Journal of Adam Ewing*, found under Frobisher's bed. He finds a hotel in nearby Bruges and works feverishly on composing his masterpiece, *Cloud Atlas Sextet*. In his final letter, having completed the work, he tells Sixsmith he will shoot himself at 5.30 AM that morning.

THE PACIFIC JOURNAL OF ADAM EWING

After a stop on the island of Raiatea in French Polynesia, the ship continues towards Honolulu. Shortly before arrival the diary breaks off due to Ewing's extreme illness, and then resumes nearly two weeks later. He recalls discovering that Dr Goose was poisoning him, and being rescued by Autua upon arrival in Honolulu. He pledges to spend the rest of his life fighting for a fairer world.

CHARACTER STUDY

THE PROTAGONIST

"Souls cross the skies o' time, Abbess'd say, like clouds crossin' skies o'the world." (p. 318)

The principle characters and narrators of each story are (mostly) linked by a comet-shaped birthmark that indicates the recurrence of a single soul in each of them. In one sense they are all the same person, living different versions of the same story, and as such can be treated as fulfilling the same role, though they do have different personalities. A minor weakness in each of their characters – naivety, pride, ambition, irresponsibility, passivity and cowardice – leads to them becoming trapped and at the mercy of others. Each of them is, however, able to keep an eye on the bigger picture, even when suffering themselves, and to act for the benefit of others. For most of the protagonists, their small kindnesses to others, carried out without thought of repayment, become instrumental in their own escapes from injustice. They learn from their experiences and conquer their personal weaknesses in pursuit of greater long-term aims, each one leaving as a result a tiny mark on the world – like a comet flashing in the night sky – which will in time become part of the story of their own soul when it returns in a new body.

THE OPPRESSOR

The oppressors, like the protagonists, are broadly the same throughout the work. In this case it is not the recurrence of a single soul, however, but the ubiquity of the worst sides of human nature that causes these different characters to act in the same way. They place zero value on human life, and consider the fulfilment of their own greed and desire to be the sole purpose of life – an aim to be pursued at any cost to other people. They deceive, imprison, manipulate and even kill the protagonists of their respective stories without pausing for thought; this decisiveness is one of their key shared traits. Making personal sacrifices for the long-term benefit of themselves and others, as the Protagonist does, is an alien concept to the Oppressor. They think only of satisfying their own base impulses, and the result of this quest for personal satisfaction is the creation of cruel and unjust worlds, and ultimately of the destruction of civilisation and the planet. However, the Oppressor does not care, or consider these consequences, because their mind is entirely focused on the present.

THE ACCOMPLICE

In each story there are also one or more characters who are sympathetic to the protagonist and help or even save them. Less proactive than the protagonists are (or become during the course of each story), they are often inspired by the actions of the protagonist to throw off their initial acceptance of the status quo. Napier in the *Half-Lives* mystery is a prime example, as he had been looking forward to a quiet retirement provided he turned a blind eye to the viciousness of Smoke and their employers, but finds himself risking and losing his own life to further Rey's cause. Sonmi~451 is helped by several characters, though they turn out to have been manipulating her all along; the very archivist to whom she is speaking, however, seems to be deeply moved by her testimony and one can infer that he has been changed for the better by his contact with Sonmi~451. With Meronym and Zachry, it is less clear who is the protagonist and who is the accomplice: Zachry is the narrator, but Meronym has the birthmark, and both overcome their own reservations to act for the benefit of the other. It is no coincidence that it is in this central story that the two types of character merge into one, with mutual cooperation the crucial factor in their escape.

THE VICTIM

Sadly, there are also victims who do not escape, from the brutalised cabin boy aboard Ewing's ship, to the numerous victims of Smoke's callous bloodlust and the tiny, doll-like fabricant tossed over a bridge in front of Sonmi~451. These examples often serve the purpose of stirring the protagonist into action, or of reminding them why their cause is just and important. They symbolise both the consequences of failure for the Protagonist and the reward for the Oppressor of maintaining the status quo. In some senses it is the pity which the protagonists feel for these characters, and their sense of rage and impotence at being unable to help them, which is the defining feature of the protagonists' personalities. Conversely, the oppressors' total disregard for their victims is the clearest demonstration of their immorality and greed. The victims are arguably victims of the novel itself, casually sacrificed by the author as a way of bringing the more central characters into sharper focus.

ANALYSIS

GENRE

In *Cloud Atlas*, David Mitchell deliberately uses six different narrative styles across multiple genres, each one appropriate to the context of its own story. The 19th-century story is written as a diary, the 1931 story as letters, the 1975 story as a typically convoluted thriller of that period, and the early 21st-century story as a film. Sonmi~451's testimony is in the form of an interview recorded in an audiovisual format, while Zachry resorts to the oldest form of story-telling – oral – to represent the cultural level to which humans have regressed by the time of his story. This has the dual effect of transporting the reader more rapidly into the new world of each story, while also allowing each narrator the opportunity to express themselves in the way that best reveals their thoughts and motives while still keeping true to the customs of the period. As the novel's setting moves into the future it takes on elements of science fiction, with two different dystopian futures described, one leading to the other. Sonmi~451's is of a near-totalitarian state in which consumer capitalism and advanced surveillance have left the general population trapped in lives of utter vacuousness, while a slave population of fabricants are more directly controlled. It is a corporate alternative to Orwell's (English author, 1903-1950) *Nineteen Eighty-Four* (1949), even down to the invented rebel organisation used to flush out and monitor would-be dissenters. Zachry's world descends into post-apocalyptic anarchy because his society is so small and fragile, in an even more distant future in which civilisation as we know it has almost completely disappeared.

STYLE

As well as writing in a style which is evocative of each setting in order to add atmosphere, Mitchell also varies the way he renders certain words. Ewing uses '&' instead of 'and' for convenience when writing his diary, and 'b—' when recording the swearing of the sailors because of his genteel sensibilities. Frobisher abbreviates names to single letters in the custom of one corresponding with a close friend to whom it is obvious who the subject under discussion is. Cavendish occasionally gives directorial instructions such as "extreme close-up, Director Lars, of Cavendish realising his fateful mistake" (p. 399) to blur the line between his first person narrative and the film it will become. By the time of Sonmi~451's interview, every 'ex' at the beginning of a word has become a single utilitarian 'x', and Zachry's dialect drops vowels and uses some new or altered words: "She list'ned close to my dreamin's, then told me they was slywise augurin's an' say-soed me to wait inside the school'ry" (p. 257). This is a constant reminder that it is not presented as a story written about Zachry, but a story being told by Zachry. Like the changes in genre, alternative spellings and stylistic variations like these serve to bring the reader closer to the mind of each character, drawing us into their worlds and making those worlds more believable.

GREED AND OPPRESSION

The most obvious recurring theme of *Cloud Atlas* is the struggle of the individual against tyranny.

On the opening page of the work, Dr Goose refers to cannibals who "engorged themselves on the weak" (p. 3), and the same character returns to this theme near the end when Goose tells Ewing that his own motto is "the weak are meat, the strong do eat" as he poisons and robs Ewing (p. 524). In every story, the protagonists face 'consumption' of one kind or another at the hands of their oppressors. Frobisher, who identifies Goose as a vampyric poisoner long before it is apparent to the reader, is himself blind to the deceptions of Ayrs and his wife as they take advantage of his destitution to feed on his talent and body respectively. Rey is continuously pursued by the murderous Smoke, facing death numerous times, and Cavendish is imprisoned in Aurora House by a combination of violent force and sedatives, where he quotes Solzhenitsyn that "unlimited power in the hands of limited people always leads to cruelty" (p. 182). Consumption becomes more literal in the final two stories, since Sonmi~451's entire race, fabricants, is destined to be recycled into basic proteins, while in a metaphorical sense their working lives are devoured in the constant service of the aptly named 'consumers'. Zachry's oppressors, the

Kona, are actual cannibals as well as plunderers and rapists; and so the story of mankind goes full cycle in *Cloud Atlas*, returning to the savagery it started with. The universality of this theme is summed up by Zachry thus:

> "The savage sat'fies his needs now. [...] His master is his will an' if his will say-soes 'Kill' he'll kill. Like fangy animals. [...] The Civ'lized got the same needs too, but he sees further. [...] His will is his slave an' if his will say'soes, 'Don't!' he won't, nay. [...] Savages an'Civilizeds ain't divvied by tribes or b'liefs or mountain ranges nay, ev'ry human is both, yay. Old'uns'd got the Smart o' gods but the savagery o' jackals an' that's what tripped the Fall." (pp. 318-319)

Throughout *Cloud Atlas*, greed is always a motivating factor, and oppression is always the result. It is a damning verdict on humanity, and the moral of the tale is that this unfettered rapacity leads to a complete destruction of society, nature and the world.

RESISTANCE

Fortunately, though Mitchell paints this bleak image of greed leading to the world becoming a partially-flooded radioactive wasteland, *Cloud Atlas* is not really about an irreversible decline, but about the importance of individual acts of resistance against this otherwise inevitable conclusion. Frobisher refuses to cooperate, and runs away to write his own music, while Cavendish simply escapes. Rey continues to fight to expose the truth about the nuclear power plant, even when her life is in danger; Sonmi~451 goes along with her scripted rebellion in order to sow the seeds of a real future revolution. On the final pages of *Cloud Atlas*, Ewing comments that "a purely predatory world shall consume itself [...] selfishness is extinction" (p. 528), but states that belief in a fair world is itself a guarantee that equality will come to pass. He imagines his father-in-law, another symbol of oppression, telling him that trying to fight human nature will mean that his "life amounted to no more than one drop in a limitless ocean" and counters in his head with the final, hope-filled words of the work: "Yet what is any ocean but a multitude of drops?" (p. 529), implying that every little act of resistance against tyranny will add up to a better world.

HUMOUR AND IRONY

The content matter is often sad, and the ulti-
mate message serious and scarcely optimistic,
but *Cloud Atlas* is not a gloomy work. Some of
the stories are more obviously humorous, such
as 'The Ghastly Ordeal of Timothy Cavendish',
which totters on the edge of absurdity from
start to finish. After throwing a smug literary
critic over a high balcony, Cavendish's thuggish
author shouts the critic's own words from the
review after him: "so who's expired in an ending
flat and inane quite beyond belief now?" (p. 152).
Cavendish's escape ends farcically with him
leaving a marked map for the carers to follow,
and then with the carers catching up to them at
a pub just inside Scotland where the senile and
hitherto useless fourth member of their escape,
Mr Meeks, suddenly invokes a Scottish nationalist
sentiment in a rich accent to summon the pub's
inhabitants to their aid. At other times Mitchell
allows his characters insight into the work itself.
Frobisher, after reading Ewing's journal, writes
to Sixsmith that there is "something shifty about
the journal's authenticity – seems too structured
for a genuine diary, and its language doesn't ring

quite true – but who would bother forging such a journal, and why?" (p. 64). Of course we know that the journal is no less artificially created and structured than Frobisher's own letters, so the irony is multi-layered.

FURTHER REFLECTION

SOME QUESTIONS TO THINK ABOUT...

- Can "one drop in a limitless ocean" (p. 529) really make a difference?
- How do the main characters grow as a result of their experiences?
- Do any of the characters earn or deserve their oppression in some way?
- Is Meronym the true protagonist of 'Sloosha's Crossin''? If so, in what ways does she become trapped in the situation?
- Who is the principle oppressor of Zachry?
- Can you find other examples of minor characters being oppressed during the course of the work?
- How do these other examples influence the protagonists?
- Is *Cloud Atlas* fundamentally an optimistic or a pessimistic work?
- In your view, does *Cloud Atlas* work convincingly as a single story?

- How does the use of the cast in the film adaptation contribute to understanding the work as a single story?

We want to hear from you!
Leave a comment on your online library
and share your favourite books on social media!

FURTHER READING

REFERENCE EDITION

- Mitchell, D. (2014) *Cloud Atlas*. London: Sceptre.

ADDITIONAL SOURCES

- David Mitchell's first novel, *Ghostwritten*, makes interesting parallel reading to *Cloud Atlas*, as it also tells a single story in several short – and at first sight disconnected – stories, and addresses many of the same themes.

ADAPTATIONS

- *Cloud Atlas*. (2012) [Film]. T. Tykwer, A. Wachowski and L. Wachowski. Dir. Germany/United States: Cloud Atlas Production, X-Filme Creative Pool, Anarchos Productions.

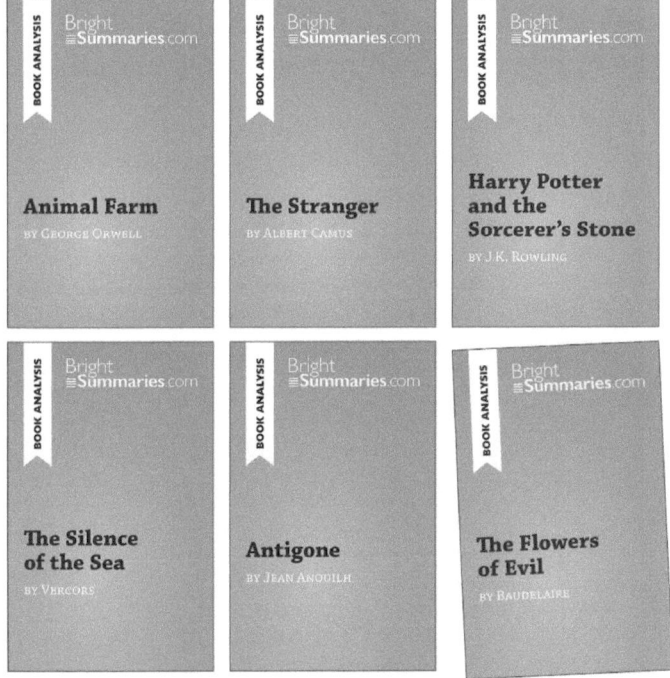

www.brightsummaries.com

Ebook EAN: 9782808014700

Paperback EAN: 9782808014717

Legal Deposit: D/2018/12603/495

Cover: © Primento

Digital conception by Primento, the digital partner of publishers.